FORTRAN IV
POCKET
HANDBOOK

DANIEL E. ALEXANDER

Department of Mechanical Engineering.
University of Washington

ANDREW C. MESSER

Aerodynamics Staff
The Boeing Company

McGraw-Hill Book Company

New York • St. Louis • San Francisco • London • Düsseldorf
Kuala Lumpur • Mexico • Montreal • Panama • Rio de Janeiro
Sydney • Toronto • Johannesburg • New Delhi • Singapore

FORTRAN IV Pocket Handbook

7 8 9 MU MU 7 9 8 7 6

Alexander, Daniel Edward.
    Fortran IV pocket handbook.

    1. FORTRAN (Computer program language) I. Messer, Andrew C., joint author. II. Title.
QA76.73.F25A43   001.6'424   72-3123
ISBN 0-07-001015-3

Preface

This *FORTRAN IV Pocket Handbook* contains a large amount of information normally found only in bulky FORTRAN text and reference books. It is written for engineers, scientists and students — from occasional computer user to skilled programmer. It may be used with any FORTRAN IV computer system. Notes are made wherever information given is in addition to ASA *Standard FORTRAN IV*. Where FORTRAN details may vary with different computer systems, reference is made to the computer system cross-reference table in Section 14.

CONTENTS

ASA Flow Chart Symbols   2

Section 1   Key Punch Machine (IBM 29) and
            Punch Cards   4

Section 2   Teletypewriter (Model 33) 16

Section 3   Constants and Variables 20

Section 4   Type Statements and Storage Allocation. 24

Section 5   Input 30

Section 6   Arithmetic Operations 38

Section 7   Library Functions 44

Section 8   Control and Transfer Statements 50

Section 9   IF 54

Section 10 DO 58

Section 11 Output 60

Section 12 Subscripted (Array) Variables 70

Section 13 Subprograms 74

Section 14 Computer System Cross-Reference . . . 84

Section 15 Glossary 86

Section 16 Index 90

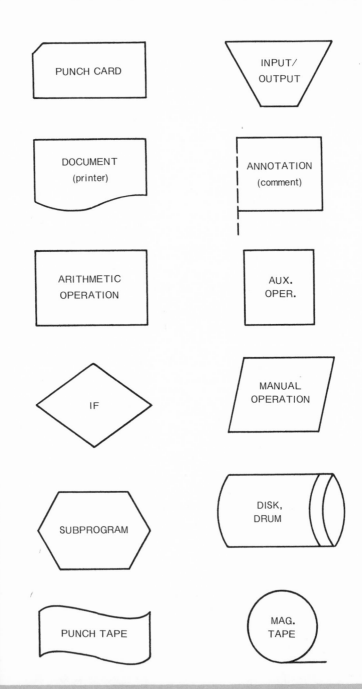

ASA FLOW CHART SYMBOLS 2

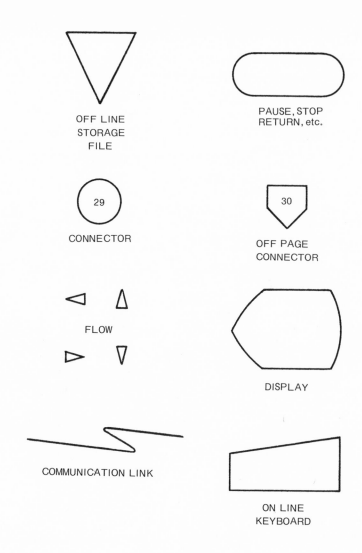

OFF LINE
STORAGE
FILE

PAUSE, STOP
RETURN, etc.

CONNECTOR

OFF PAGE
CONNECTOR

FLOW

DISPLAY

COMMUNICATION LINK

ON LINE
KEYBOARD

ASA FLOW CHART SYMBOLS

1

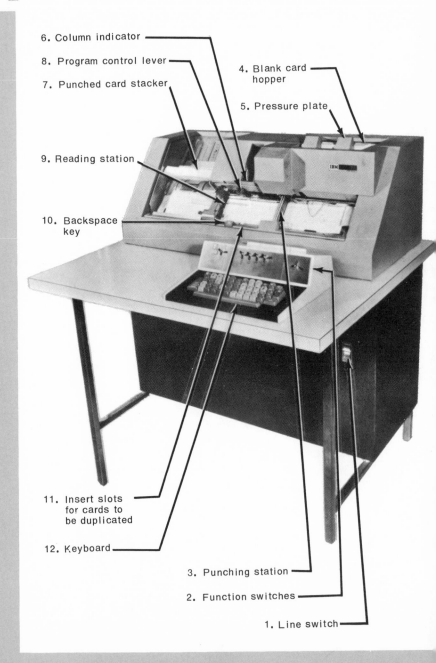

6. Column indicator

8. Program control lever

7. Punched card stacker

4. Blank card hopper

5. Pressure plate

9. Reading station

10. Backspace key

11. Insert slots for cards to be duplicated

12. Keyboard

3. Punching station

2. Function switches

1. Line switch

KEY PUNCH MACHINE (IBM 29)   4

1. **Line switch** — turns machine ON & OFF (no warm-up required)

2. **Function switches** — (see also figure on page 6)

   AUTO SKIP DUP   — activates automatic skip and duplicate DRUM CARD functions

   PROG SEL 1-2   — selects initial DRUM CARD program to be used with a new card

   AUTO FEED   — causes release, feed, and register to occur each time column 80 passes the punching station.

   PRINT   — activates the card printing mechanism (leftmost + − and 0's are suppressed in numeric DRUM CARD fields)

   LZ PRINT   — includes printing of leftmost + − and 0's with PRINT on

   CLEAR   — causes 3 cycles of release and register, clearing stations of cards

3. **Punching station** — punches new card

4. **Blank card hopper** — holds up to 500 new cards (12 edge up)

5. **Pressure plate** — maintains card alignment in hopper

6. **Column indicator** — also location of DRUM CARD and jammed card release lever

7. **Punched card stacker** — receives up to 500 punched cards

8. **Program control lever** — turn ON (left side down) to use DRUM CARD program, must be OFF to remove drum

9. **Reading station** — reads cards to be duplicated

10. **Backspace key** — continues to backspace as long as it is held down

11. **Insert slots for card to be duplicated** — allows manual card insertion.

12. **Keyboard** — see next page

1

KEYBOARD AND FUNCTION SWITCHES

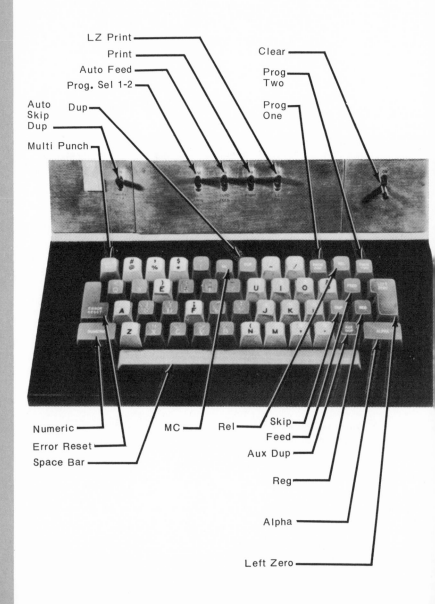

KEY	FUNCTION WITH DRUM CARD	FUNCTION WITHOUT DRUM CARD
ERROR RESET	unlocks keyboard after an interlock.	
MULT PCH	allows upper register characters to be punched in the same column, regardless of the register selected.	Same
		as
		with
FEED	feeds card from hopper to card bed, also registers first card.	drum
		card
REG	registers card at column 1 in punching and/or reading station.	
NUMERIC	causes shift to upper register when alphabetic field is programmed.	causes shift to upper register (keyboard normally in lower reg).
DUP	causes duplication of entire field (20 col/sec).	causes duplication as long as key is held (10 col/sec).
REL	same as without drum card, but any programmed duplication after REL key is depressed will still take place.	advances card in punch station to read station, and card in read station to base of card stacker.
SKIP	causes skip of entire field.	skips one space.
MC	activates master card functions.	
PROG ONE (PROG TWO)	selects upper (lower) DRUM CARD program, also causes feed cycle if a card is not registered, stops program if no program one (two) punched.	No
		function
		without
LEFT ZERO	causes punching of stored data into a left-zero field.	drum
AUX DUP	requires master card on auxiliary drum (behind DRUM CARD) — causes duplication from the master card.	card
ALPHA	causes shift to lower register when numeric field is programmed.	

DRUM CARD

Location of DRUM CARD
in the machine

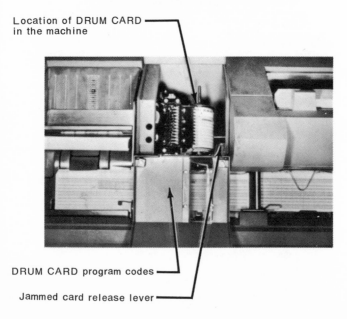

DRUM CARD program codes

Jammed card release lever

KEY PUNCH MACHINE (IBM 29) 8

DRUM CARD: controls automatic functions of the keypunch machine for punching large numbers of cards with the same format.

It is activated by the program control lever.

Two programs are available on one drum card. Program One uses codes in the top 6 rows, and program Two uses the bottom 6 rows. The initial program to be used when a new card is fed is selected by the PROG SEL ONE-TWO switch; however, the program may be changed any other time by using the PROG ONE and PROG TWO keys.

Each row in each program controls a specific function which may be used independently or together with other functions as required.

DRUM CARD PROGRAM CODES:

PROG ONE Code	PROG TWO Code	Function	Use
12	4	field designation	**blank** in first column of each field, **12 code** in remaining columns of each field.
11	5	start AUTO SKIP	first column of field only— causes machine to skip to start of next field.
0	6	start AUTO DUP	first column of field only — causes machine to duplicate data from the previous card. AUTO DUP stops at beginning of next field. The keyboard will interlock at a blank in a numeric field.
1	7	punch alphabetic	every column where required — causes keyboard to shift to lower (alphabetic) register. Note: Keyboard is normally in the upper (numeric) register when using the automatic functions.
2	8	8 col. L-Z field	first column of numeric field of corresponding width — causes significant digits to be placed in storage (not punched). Depressing the LEFT ZERO key then causes the digits to be punched (16 col/sec), right justified in the field, with zero fill to the left. The ERROR RESET key clears the storage if required.
3	9	7 " " "	
2,3	8,9	6 " " "	
1,2	7,8	5 " " "	
1,3	7,9	4 " " "	
1,2,3	7,8,9	3 " " "	

1

PUNCH CARD CODE — A typical punched card code arrangement is shown opposite. Different computer systems may use different code arrangements.

Combinations of codes for the DRUM CARD may be created by MULT PCH + − 0 thru 9 or by normal use of any other character that is made up of the required codes.

ASA STANDARD FORTRAN IV CHARACTER SET

Note: letter Ø, l
number 0, 1

A to Z	alphabetic	} alphanumeric
0 to 9	numeric	

	blank	
=	equals	
+	plus	
−	minus	
*	asterisk	
/	slash	} special characters
(	left parenthesis	
)	right parenthesis	
,	comma	
.	decimal point	
$	currency symbol	

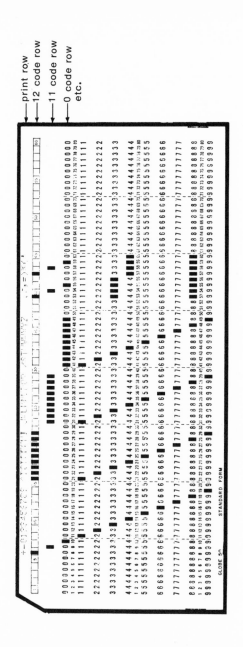

—print row
—12 code row
—11 code row
—0 code row
etc.

PUNCH CARDS

FORTRAN STATEMENT AND DATA PUNCH CARDS

Statement numbers — (integers up to 99999^v) in columns $1-5$, may be used as necessary with any FORTRAN statement except END statement. Each *must be unique* in the program or subprogram.

FORTRAN statements — in columns $7-72$, if more space is required continue on next card in columns $7-72$ and punch *any* character (except zero) in column 6. Up to 19^v continuation cards are permitted.

Identification — codes may be punched in columns $73-80$ of *any* card, except data cards, for the personal use of the programmer and are not computed.

Comments — may be punched in columns $2-80$, with "C" in column 1.

Data — may be punched in columns $1-80$.

---

^{v} Varies with different computer systems (see Sec. 14)

(80 edge)

Top (12 edge)

Bottom (9 edge)

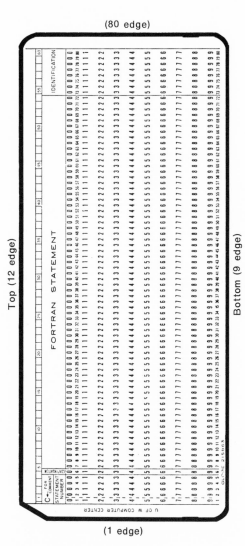

(1 edge)

PUNCH CARDS

1

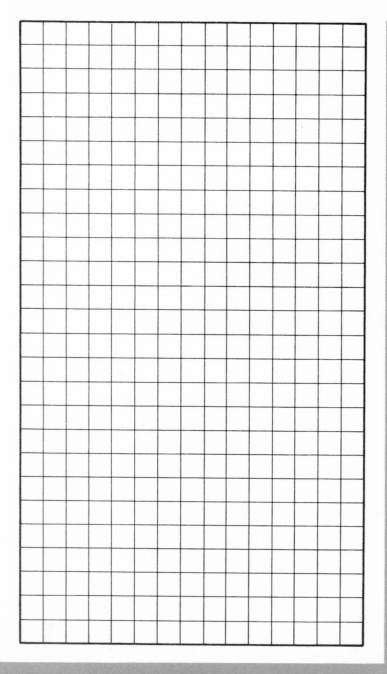

NOTES

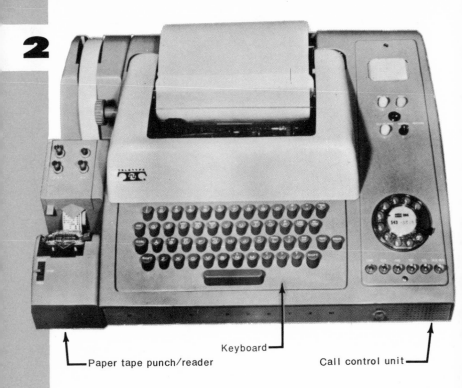

Paper tape punch/reader   Keyboard   Call control unit

CALL CONTROL UNIT

BRK-RLS	lights when a BREAK signal has been sent or received. Must then be pressed to unlock keyboard.
FDX (REST)	switch supresses printing while transmitting to allow full duplex operation.
OUT OF SERV	light indicates terminal has been placed out of service.
NORMAL-RESTORE	switch — point to OUT OF SERV light to remove terminal from telephone service — turn to RESTORE then release to place terminal back in telephone service.
AUTO ANS	selects automatic answering function (if installed).
Dial	standard telephone dial.
ORIG	turns machine on and obtains a dial tone.
CLEAR	turns machine off and clears telephone connection.
ANS	Lights to indicate an incoming call, depress to answer — turns machine on.

TELETYPEWRITER (MODEL 33)   16

TST	Used for maintenance.
LCL	turns machine on without using telephone connection.
BUZ-RLS	stops "low paper supply" warning buzzer.
Loudspeaker	telephone receiver loudspeaker with volume control — located under key shelf.

PAPER TAPE PUNCH

ON	Engages tape puncher. Teletypewriter operation is also punched in paper tape.
OFF	disengages tape puncher.
REL	releases feed rollers for threading tape.
B SP	backspaces tape one space.

PAPER TAPE READER

MANUAL START	starts paper tape reader (spring-loaded to AUTO position).
AUTO	allows paper tape reader to start from transmitted signal.
MANUAL STOP	stops paper tape reader (reader also stops when the end of the tape is reached or at an X OFF).
FREE	releases drive sprocket to allow manual movement of the tape.

KEYBOARD

Alphanumeric Keys	Letters (capital only), numbers and : — ; , . / shown on the lower portion of the keytops, are printed when depressed.
SHIFT	causes special characters ! '' # $ % & ' ( ) * = — @ + ↑ < > ? shown on the upper portion of the keytops, to be printed when the key is depressed.
CTRL	causes the following special functions, shown on the upper portion of the keytops, to be obtained when the key is depressed:
RU	use varies.
X OFF	when punched in paper tape will stop the tape reader.
WRU	(who are you?) causes distant station to give its automatic answer-back identifier.
EOT	(end of transmission) used as a disconnect.
TAPE	starts paper tape at a distant station.
~~TAPE~~	stops paper tape at a distant station.
BELL	signals distant station.
TAB	use varies.
VT	use varies.
FORM	use varies.
HERE IS	sends your automatic answer-back identifier.
RETURN	returns type-head to left margin.
LINE FEED	advances paper.

2

RUB OUT	nonprinting, deletes backspaced characters in paper tape, used twice to begin each line (after RETURN, LINE FEED) and twice after any CTRL functions are used.
REPT	causes continuous repetition of any key held simultaneously.
BREAK	used to interrupt incoming transmission.
ESC	use varies, sometimes used in computer operation instead of BREAK.

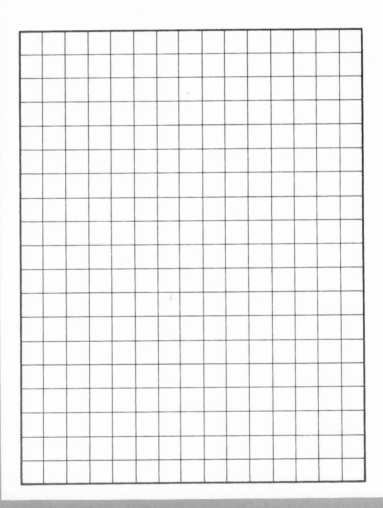

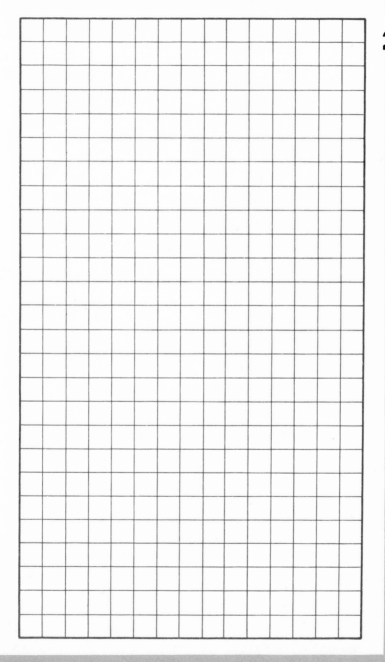

NOTES

COMPARISON OF NUMBER SYSTEMS

MAGNITUDE	BASE TEN DECIMAL	BASE TWO BINARY	BASE EIGHT OCTAL	BASE SIXTEEN HEXADECIMAL
2^{-16}	.0000152587890625	.0000000000000001	.000005	.0001
	.000030517578125	.000000000000001	.00001	.000125
	.00006103515625	.00000000000001	.000025	.00025
	.0001220703125	.0000000000001	.00005	.0005
	.000244140625	.000000000001	.0001	.001
2^{-10}	.00048828125	.00000000001	.00025	.00125
	.0009765625	.0000000001	.0005	.0025
	.001953125	.000000001	.001	.005
	.00390625	.00000001	.0025	.01
	.0078125	.0000001	.005	.0125
2^{-5}	.015625	.000001	.01	.025
	.03125	.00001	.025	.05
	.0625	.0001	.05	.1
	.125	.001	.1	.125
	.25	.01	.25	.25
2^{-1}	.5	.1	.5	.5
	0	0	0	0
2^{0}	1	1	1	1
	2	10	2	2
	3	11	3	3
2^{2}	4	100	4	4
	5	101	5	5
	6	110	6	6
	7	111	7	7
2^{3}	8	1000	10	8
	9	1001	11	9
	10	1010	12	A
	11	1011	13	B
	12	1100	14	C
	13	1101	15	D
	14	1110	16	E
	15	1111	17	F
	16	10000	20	10
2^{5}	32	100000	40	20
	64	1000000	100	40
	128	10000000	200	80
	256	100000000	400	100
	512	1000000000	1000	200
2^{10}	1024	10000000000	2000	400
	2048	100000000000	4000	800
	4096	1000000000000	10000	1000
	8192	10000000000000	20000	2000
	16384	100000000000000	40000	4000
	32768	1000000000000000	100000	8000
2^{16}	65536	10000000000000000	200000	10000
π	3.1416	11.001001000	3.11	3.243
e	2.7182	10.101101111110	2.5576	2.B7E1

Type	Field	Constant	Variable
		neg. requires − sign pos. optional + sign	name consists of 1-6[v] alphanumeric characters starting with alphabetic
CØMPLEX	G, F or E	two REAL numbers up to 7[v] digits each in real or exponential form: CMPLX (27.5,-.133E1 means 27.5-1.33i	requires TYPE statement
DØUBLE PRECISIØN	D	FLOATING POINT number up to 16[v] digits with or without decimal followed by exponent: 13.D+1 or 13D1 means 130.0	requires TYPE statement
REAL	F	up to 7[v] digits, with decimal. 21.753 called FLOATING POINT	name starts with A-H, Ø-Z, or TYPE statement required
EXPØNENTIAL	E	same as REAL, with or without decimal followed by exponent: 21.7E-2 or 217E-3 means 0.217	same as REAL
INTEGER	I	up to 10[v] digits, no decimal, 21753 called FIXED POINT	name starts with I-N or TYPE statement required
[n]ØCTAL	Ø	6-20 digits preceded by the letter Ø, Ø307476 or 1-20 digits followed by the letter B of the digit set 0-7: 124B	same as INTEGER
[n]HEXADECIMAL	Z	up to 8 digits of the set 0-9 and A-F preceded by the character Z:ZA70F	any variable name
LØGICAL	L	values .TRUE. or .FALSE.	requires TYPE statement
ALPHAMERIC HOLLERITH	A or [n]R	1-10[v] characters, preceded by wH, where w is the total number of characters including blanks (more than 10[v] characters requires DIMENSION and DATA statements)	any VARIABLE name, INTEGER name if manipulation is to be performed MONTH(7) =4HJULY YEAR = 5HTIGER

[n] Not included in ASA Standard FORTRAN IV
[v] Varies with different computer systems (see Sec. 14)

CONSTANTS AND VARIABLES

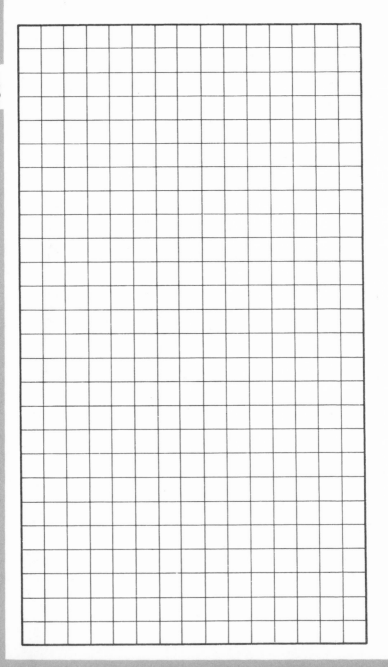

3

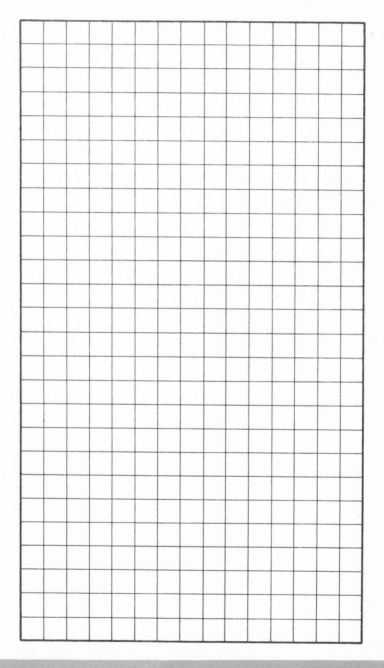

NOTES

Type	Use
CØMPLEX	variable names listed will be computed as complex numbers made up of two REAL numbers representing the real and imaginary parts EXAMPLE: CØMPLEX ZETA,J(2,3)
DØUBLE PRECISIØN	variable names listed will be computed using a double number of REAL digits EXAMPLE: DØUBLE PRECISIØN X,LENGTH,A(2)
REAL	variable names listed become REAL regardless of first letter EXAMPLE: REAL K45,MHØ,N(12),J
INTEGER	variable names listed become INTEGER regardless of first letter EXAMPLE: INTEGER DEL,TABLE (15,5),B,YEAR
LØGICAL	variable names listed can assume only the values .TRUE. or .FALSE. EXAMPLE: LØGICAL A,J,K(10)
EXTERNAL	lists subprogram names that will be used as actual arguments when calling other subprograms (may NOT be subscripted) EXAMPLE: EXTERNAL INTØM,RECHK

Restrictions

1. An array name may have its dimensions specified in a Type Statement, but it then may NOT have its dimensions specified in a DIMENSIØN or CØMMØN statement.

2. Type Statement MUST precede the first appearance of the listed variables in any executable statement. It is preferable to place all Type Statements prior to all executable statements[v].

3. Once the type of a variable is specified, it may not be changed in the program.

4. A variable name may be listed in only ONE Type Statement, EXCEPT that a variable name listed in an EXTERNAL Type Statement may be listed in ONE other Type Statement.

---

[v]Varies with different computer systems (see Sec. 14)

TYPE STATEMENTS

Statement	Use
DIMENSIØN	specifies name and storage space required for subscripted data and arrays 3 dimensions per array maximum in most systems. (see Sec. 14).

EXAMPLE:

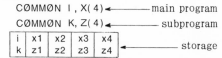

variable names ⟶
DIMENSIØN LISTA (900),BØX(4,4,4)
storage dimensions ⟋
(separated by commas, enclosed in parentheses)

Blank CØMMØN

places data from main and subprograms in the same storage locations. Arrays may be dimensioned, but then NOT elsewhere. Types MUST correspond.

EXAMPLE:

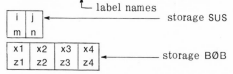

CØMMØN I , X(4)◀——————main program

CØMMØN K, Z(4)◀——————subprogram

i	x1	x2	x3	x4
k	z1	z2	z3	z4

◀—————— storage

Labeled CØMMØN

same as CØMMØN but provides *several* blocks of CØMMØN storage. Label names must be identical in main and subprograms and surrounded by slashes. Types MUST correspond.

EXAMPLE:

CØMMØN /SUS/I , J/BØB/X(4)◀—main prog

CØMMØN /SUS/M, N ◀——————subprogram 1

CØMMØN /BØB/Z (4)◀—————— subprogram 2

└— label names

i	j
m	n

◀—————————— storage SUS

x1	x2	x3	x4
z1	z2	z3	z4

◀—————— storage BØB

EQUIVALENCE

allows different variable or array names to refer to same storage locations — *within same program only*. Arrays must be dimensioned in a DIMENSIØN statement. With subscripted variables and arrays, equivalencing one set equivalences all adjacent sets. Types MUST correspond.

EXAMPLE:

EQUIVALENCE (X,Y,Z), (ØHM,RES)

x	ohm
y	res
z	

◀—— storage

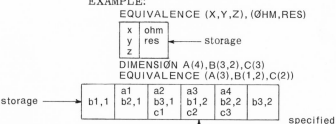

DIMENSIØN A(4),B(3,2),C(3)
EQUIVALENCE (A(3),B(1,2),C(2))

storage ⟶

	a1	a2	a3	a4	
b1,1	b2,1	b3,1	b1,2	b2,2	b3,2
		c1	c2	c3	

specified point

Statement	Use
DATA	specifies initial values for listed variables *prior* to program execution. Variable names are listed (separated by commas) and followed by their corresponding values (separated by commas, enclosed in slashes).

EXAMPLE:

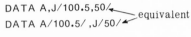

DATA A,J/100.5,50/ equivalent
DATA A/100.5/,J/50/

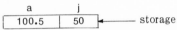

a	j
100.5	50	◄——— storage

Note: data must correspond in TYPE to variables listed.

Array name implies entire array.
EXAMPLE:

    DIMENSIØN B(4)
    DATA B/1.0,1.5,2.0,2.5/

Subscripted array name indicates single array element.
EXAMPLE:

    DATA C(27,4,1)/5.6/

Listed variables with the *same* value may use the form n*v enclosed in slashes, where n is the number of times value v is repeated.
EXAMPLE:

    DATA D,E,F,G,H/1.0,3*2.0,5.0/

d	e	f	g	h
1.0	2.0	2.0	2.0	5.0	◄— storage

Single index implied DØ may be used for arrays or segments of arrays. Indexing parameter must be integer constant.
EXAMPLE:

    DIMENSIØN A(5,6)
    DATA (A(K),K=1,14)/10*5.5,4*6.2/
    DATA (A(K),K=15,30)/16*9.7/

Statement	Use
DATA	Alphameric data may be specified.

EXAMPLE:

DATA MØ/4HJULY/

The variable must be dimensioned for long character strings — one storage space for each 10 characters (number varies with different computer systems).

EXAMPLE:

DIMENSIØN DAY (2)
DATA DAY/15HTUESDAY 27 JULY/

4

Statement	Use
BLØCK DATA	subprogram to enter data into labeled CØMMØN

storage. Contains *only* the BLOCK DATA statement, TYPE, DIMENSIØN, CØMMØN, DATA, and END statements. CØMMØN statements must include all elements in the common blocks listed. DATA statements may define only elements listed in CØMMØN statement, but need not include list names.

EXAMPLE:

BLØCK DATA
INTEGER Y
DIMENSIØN Y(4)
CØMMØN/DDD/Y
DATA Y/68,69,70,71/
END

[n]NAMELIST   permits input and output of several variables by calling one name, without format statement. Fields are generated as required NAMELIST names are surrounded by slashes, followed by variable or array names which are separated by commas.

EXAMPLE:

    DIMENSIØN K(8)
    NAMELIST /JANET/A,B,ØHM,K/TIM/I,J

    . . .
    READ (5,JANET)   note: see
    . . .   input card
    WRITE (6,JANET)   layout below

    . . .
    READ (5,TIM)

    . . .
    WRITE (6,TIM)

    . . .

[n]NAMELIST DATA CARD FORMAT

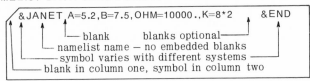

```
&JANET A=5.2,B=7.5,OHM=10000.,K=8*2        &END
```
blank   blanks optional
namelist name — no embedded blanks
symbol varies with different systems
blank in column one, symbol in column two

```
&TIM I=40000,J=100 & END
```

[n] Not included in ASA Standard FORTRAN IV

[v]NOTE: Some compilers require that type and storage allocation statements appear prior to the first executable statement and in the following order:

           Type Statements
           EXTERNAL
           DIMENSIØN
           CØMMØN
           EQUIVALENCE
           DATA

[v]Varies with different computer systems (see Sec. 14)

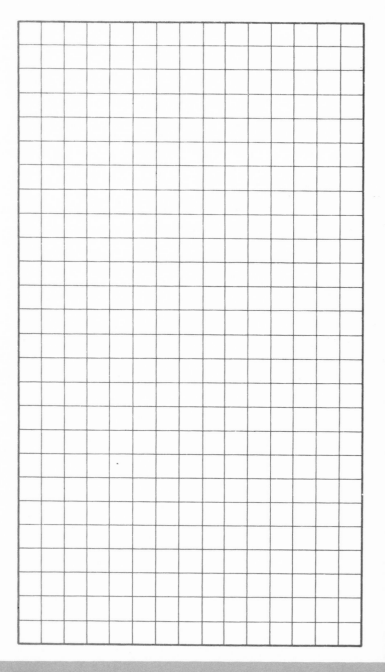

NOTES

INPUT DATA — may be placed in storage by:

1. Executable statements:

    A = 1.05
    I = 27
    BAR = A**2 + 42.16
    DAY(3) = 7HTUESDAY   **Note**: 10^V characters maximum
                                 in each alphameric
                                 storage location.

2. DATA statement: see Sec. 4

3. Unformatted READ statement: see Sec. 8

4. Variable format READ statement: see page 37

5. Fixed format READ statement (parentheses as shown):

    ⌐ input device number (see page 31)

             ⌐variables to be read in (separated by
              commas — spaces ignored)
              (implied DØ — see Sec. 12)

READ (5,300) A, DIA(2,1), JBAR
                         statement number

300   FØRMAT (2F20.6,I10)
                     coded instructions on how input data
                     will be read. (Fields must be separated
                     by commas and enclosed in paren-
                     theses — spaces ignored)

Note:

1. Variables and fields MUST correspond in type.

2. If the number of variables listed in the READ statement is *less* than the number of fields listed in the FORMAT statement the extra fields are ignored.

3. If the number of variables listed in the READ statement *exceeds* the number of fields listed in the FORMAT statement, the FORMAT statement is used again from its beginning and the remaining variables are read from the next data cards (or tape records).

EXAMPLE:
This pair of statements:

     READ (5,400) A,E,I,O,U,L,W ◄——— 7 variables
400 FØRMAT (2F10.2,I5) ◄——————— 3 fields

Will input from 3 cards: A,E,I ◄———

27.3	14.4	5
68.0	7.66	20
−5.1425		

O,U,L ◄———
W ◄———

|◄—— 10 ——►|◄—— 10 ——►|◄— 5 —►|

^{V}Varies with different computer systems (see Sec. 14)

INPUT RULES When placing data in input fields:

1. ONLY *characters* within the specified field width "w" are read — others are ignored.

2. *Signs* may be omitted for positive numbers.

3. *Decimals* may be *omitted* in F, E, D and G fields since the computer will insert the decimal according to the "d" in the field specification. Data MUST be *right justified* to the end of the field or to the beginning of the exponent, because blanks are interpreted as zeros.

4. *Decimals* may be *included* in F, E, D and G fields causing the "d" in the field specification to be overridden — right justification is NOT required.

5. *Exponents* may be included or omitted in F, E, D and G fields (exponent assumed zero when omitted) and may be written with or without the letter "E" or "D" (exponent sign may NOT be omitted if exponent letter is omitted). Blanks are optional and are interpreted as zeros. Exponents must be right adjusted.

6. SCALE FACTOR changes value by 10^S in F, E, D and G fields when exponent E or D is omitted and is ignored when exponent is included.

7. *Integers* MUST be right justified, because blanks are interpreted as zeros.

8. COMPLEX data requires two E, F or G input fields for each variable read, one for the real part followed by one for the imaginary part.

9. *ONLY* the first 7^V REAL significant digits (16^V DØUBLE PRECISIØN, etc.) will be placed in storage, regardless of the number of digits read. The value may NOT exceed the maximum allowed for the type[v] or an error condition results.

10. LØGICAL data is read as .TRUE. if the first non-blank character is "T" and .FALSE. if the first non-blank character is "F" or the field is blank.

11. All *characters* including blanks in an A or R field are considered as input data and are placed in storage as read (left justified for A fields, right justified for R fields) up to the character limit for alphameric storage (10 characters — number varies in different systems), then the rightmost 10 characters are stored.

Note: See examples of these Input Rules on pages 34 and 35.

[v] Varies with different computer systems (see Sec. 14)

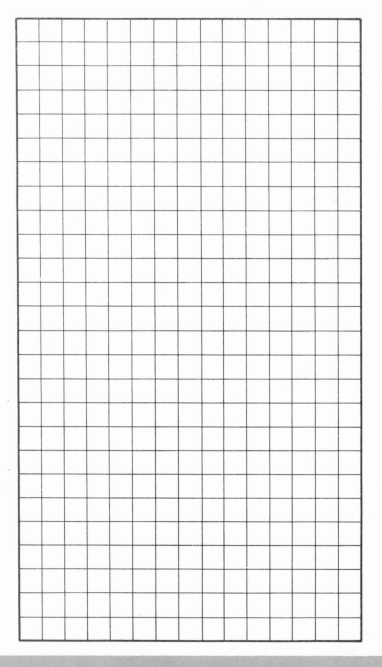

NOTES

Rule	Input Specification	Data	Value to be placed in storage
1.	F10.4	-322.19|27	-322.1900
	F10.4	-322.1927	+22.19270
	F10.4	-322.1927	+0.000000
2.	F10.4	322.1927	+322.1927
3.	F10.4	3221927	+322.1927
	F10.4	-322192700	-32219.27
	F10.4	-3221927	-32219.27
	E10.4	3221927E 0	+322.1927
4.	F10.4	-.32219270	-.3221927
	E10.4	.3221927E2	+32.21927
5.	E10.4	3221927	+322.1927
	F10.4	3221927E-2	+3.221927
	G10.4	.3221927+3	+322.1927
	D10.4	3221927D2	$+322.1927000000000 \times 10^{20}$
6.	2PE10.4	32.21927	+3221.927
	2PF10.4	32.21927E0	+32.21927
	-2PG10.4	32.21927	+.3221927
	-2PD10.4	32.21927D0	+32.21927000000000

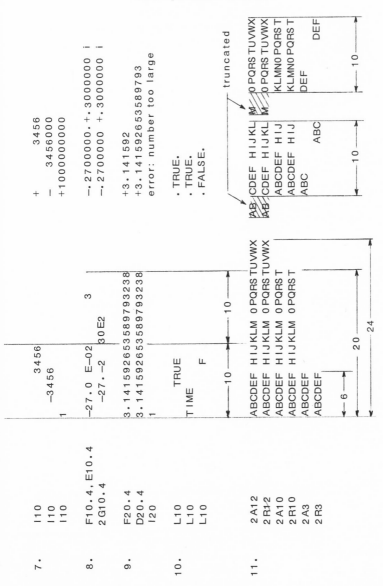

	Format	Input	Result
7.	I10	3456	+ 3456
	I10	-3456	- 3456000
	I10	1	+1000000000
8.	F10.4,E10.4	-27.0 E-02 3	-.2700000.+.3000000 i
	2G10.4	-27.-2 30E2	-.2700000 +.3000000 i
9.	F20.4	3.14159265358979 3238	+3.141592
	D20.4	3.14159265358979 3238	+3.14159265358979 3
	I20	1	error: number too large
10.	L10	TRUE	.TRUE.
	L10	F	.TRUE.
	L10	TIME	.FALSE.
11.	2A12	ABCDEF HIJKLM 0PQRS TUVWX	AB CDEF HIJKL M 0PQRS TUVWX (truncated)
	2R12	ABCDEF HIJKLM 0PQRS TUVWX	AB CDEF HIJKL M 0PQRS TUVWX
	2A10	ABCDEF HIJKLM 0PQRS T	ABCDEF HIJ KLMN0 PQRS T
	2R10	ABCDEF HIJKLM 0PQRS T	ABCDEF HIJ KLMN0 PQRS T
	2A3	ABCDEF	ABC DEF
	2R3	ABCDEF	ABC DEF

HOLLERITH FIELD

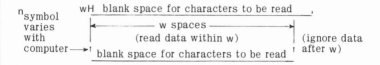

n_{symbol}
varies
with
computer

wH blank space for characters to be read ____ ,

|← —————— w spaces —————— →|
(read data within w)
blank space for characters to be read '
(ignore data after w)

Note: Characters read into the above fields will be stored in the FØRMAT statement and may be reproduced as output by using that FØRMAT statement with a WRITE statement.

EXAMPLE:

These 3 statements: 10   Will input from this card:
                        ⟵ spaces
    READ(5, 100)   MY SON JOHN WENT TO SCHOOL
100 FØRMAT(5X, 10H   )|← 5 →|←—10 —→|

    . . . . .
    WRITE(6, 100)   And produce this printed output:

                                   N JOHN WEN

n**TAB FIELD**   Tw   (starts the NEXT field at column w)

BLANK FIELD wX   (gives w columns where no data is read)

NEW RECORD slash (/)

The slash causes skipping to the next card (or tape record) whenever it appears in a FØRMAT statement between fields, at the beginning or end of the statement; commas are not needed; it does not apply to succeeding input specifications; there is no limit on the number of repetitions per statement.

EXAMPLE:

300   FØRMAT (//4F10.4/I15/)

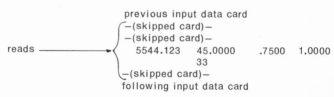

                    previous input data card
                  ⎧ —(skipped card)—
                  ⎪ —(skipped card)—
    reads ———————⎨   5544.123   45.0000   .7500   1.0000
                  ⎪   33
                  ⎩ —(skipped card)—
                    following input data card

n Not included in ASA Standard FORTRAN

VARIABLE FORMAT READ & WRITE

Provides the capability of reading in FORMAT specifications to be used with other READ or WRITE statements. The FORMAT specifications are stored in single dimensioned alphameric arrays, and are in the same form as fixed FORMAT specifications. Array must have INTEGER name.

EXAMPLE:

These statements:

```
          DIMENSION LAYOUT (8)
          . . . . .
          READ (5,100) LAYOUT
100       FORMAT (8A10)
```
⟵ INTEGER array name
```
          . . . . .
          READ (5,LAYOUT) HOURS,RATE,NUM
          . . . . .
          WRITE(6,LAYOUT) HOURS,RATE,NUM
```

Will input from these data cards:

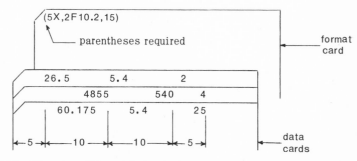

format card

parentheses required

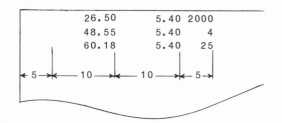

data cards

And will produce this printed output:

```
          26.50      5.40 2000
          48.55      5.40    4
          60.18      5.40   25
```
←5→|←—10—→|←—10—→|←5→

EQUAL SIGN:
(=)

Means: "replaces" or "is destructively replaced by the value of"

Use: single variable = any valid expression of variables & constants

EXAMPLE:

A=A+100.0 means the new value stored at address A is now equal to the old value stored at address A plus 100.0 or A is destructively replaced by the value of A plus 100.0

Alternate Use: Mode assignment, i.e. converting REAL to INTEGER, INTEGER to REAL, etc. (see Table 1, page 40).

EXAMPLE:

I=A   if A=10.275   the new I=10
A=I   if I =10   the new A=10.0

MODE (type):

Generally arithmetic operations should be either ALL REAL, ALL INTEGER, etc. (see Sec. 3) or the program will be rejected for a "MIXED MODE" error. Special cases are permitted (see Tables 2 and 3, page 41).

EXAMPLE:

same mode   B + 35.6
same mode   J * 2 + 7
mixed mode L*W*H
mixed mode P/2 − 45.8

PRIORITY:

All operations are executed in order of priority. Operations having the same priority are executed in order of appearance from left to right.

FORTRAN OPERATION PRIORITY

( )	parentheses	1	all operations within ( ) are executed first
**	exponent (power)	2	A**B means a^b A**(1./B) means $\sqrt[b]{a}$ A**(−2.) means $\dfrac{1}{a^2}$ integers may be used as positive powers ex: A**2 (see Table 2, page 41).
*	multiply	3	A*B means ab A*(−B) means $a(-b)$
/	divide	3	A/B means $\dfrac{a}{b}$ A/(−B) means $\dfrac{a}{-b}$ integer fractions will truncate ex: 10/4 will truncate to 2 $\frac{1}{2}$ will truncate to 0 etc.
+	add	4	A+B means $a+b$
−	subtract	4	A−B means $a-b$
logical operators		5-8	see Sec 9

EXAMPLES OF PRIORITY

FORTRAN STATEMENT	ALGEBRAIC MEANING
A = R*X**(3.+Y)/(T−FLOAT(J))	$a = \dfrac{rx^{3+y}}{t-j}$
A = R*X**3.+Y/T−FLOAT(J)	$a = rx^3 + \dfrac{y}{t} - j$
I = (J−N**(2+L))/(IFIX(X)*M)	$i = \dfrac{j - n^{2+L}}{xm}$
I = (J−N)**2+L/IFIX(X)*M	$i = (j-n)^2 + \dfrac{Lm}{x}$

The following tables show valid MODE ASSIGNMENT & REPLACE-MENT operations and the MODE (type) of the result. Shaded operations are non-ASA, but are permitted in some systems[v].

MODE (type) in order of dominance: C — CØMPLEX
D — DØUBLE PRECISIØN
F — REAL
I — INTEGER
L — LØGICAL

TABLE 1   MODE ASSIGNMENT   (Equal sign)

	Variable (left of =)	Expression (right of =)				
			C	D	F	I	L

		C	D	F	I	L
	C	C	C	C	C	C
	D	D	D	D	D	D
=	F	F	F	F	F	F
	I	I	I	I	I	I
	L	L	L	L	L	L

Example: I = A
(if A=10.275
the new I=10)

Note: [n]1. If a CØMPLEX expression is assigned to a non-CØMPLEX variable, the real part is assigned. If a non-CØMPLEX expression is assigned to a CØMPLEX variable, it is assigned to the real part.

2. If a DØUBLE PRECISIØN expression is assigned to a non-D.P. variable, the most significant part is assigned. If a non-D.P. expression is assigned to a D.P. variable, it is assigned to the most significant part.

[n]3. If a LØGICAL expression is assigned to a non-LØGICAL variable, the variable will have the value 0 if the expression is false, and —0 if true. If a non-LØGICAL expression is assigned to a LØGICAL variable, the variable will be .F. if the expression is 0, and .T. if ≠ 0.

[n] Not included in ASA Standard FORTRAN IV
[v] Varies with different computer systems (see Sec. 14)

TABLE 2   MODE REPLACEMENT (Exponentiation)

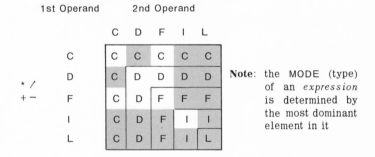

	C	D	F	I	L
C	–	–	–	C	–
D	–	D	D	D	–
F	–	D	F	F	–
I	–	–	–	I	–
L	–	–	–	I	–

(– not permitted)

Note: negative numbers may ONLY be raised to INTEGER powers

TABLE 3   MODE REPLACEMENT (Arithmetic operators)

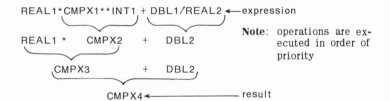

1st Operand   2nd Operand

	C	D	F	I	L
C	C	C	C	C	C
D	C	D	D	D	D
F	C	D	F	F	F
I	C	D	F	I	I
L	C	D	F	I	L

Note: the MODE (type) of an *expression* is determined by the most dominant element in it

EXAMPLE OF MODE REPLACEMENT

REAL1*CMPX1**INT1 + DBL1/REAL2 ←—expression

REAL1 *   CMPX2   +   DBL2

CMPX3   +   DBL2

CMPX4 ←——————— result

Note: operations are executed in order of priority

6

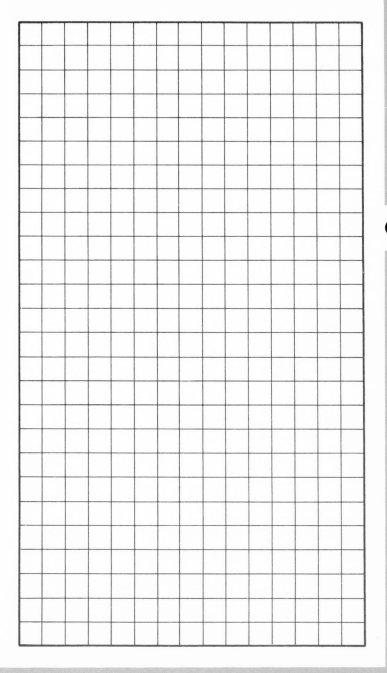

43

The following tables list, by type of result, the library of built-in functions usually found in large FORTRAN IV systems. Arguments are indicated by:

C   represents any CØMPLEX variable or valid complex expression.

D & P represent any DØUBLE PRECISIØN variables or valid D.P. expressions.

A & B represent any REAL variables or valid real expressions.

I & J represent any INTEGER variables or valid integer expressions.

COMPLEX FUNCTIONS

	CALL	FUNCTION
	CSQRT(C)	square root
n	CCBRT(C)	cube root
	CEXP(C)	exponential e^c
	CLØG(C)	natural logarithm
	CSIN(C)	trigonometric sine
	CCØS(C)	trigonometric cosine
n	CTAN(C)	trigonometric tangent
n	CSINH(C)	hyperbolic sine
n	CCØSH(C)	hyperbolic cosine
n	CTANH(C)	hyperbolic tangent
	CMPLX(A,B)	convert real to complex $A + iB$
	CØNJG(C)	complex conjugate
n	CABS(C)	magnitude

DOUBLE PRECISION FUNCTIONS

	CALL	FUNCTION	REMARKS
	DABS(D)	absolute value	
	DSQRT(D)	square root	$D \geqslant 0$
n	DCBRT(D)	cube root	
	DEXP(D)	exponential e^d	
	DLØG(D)	natural logarithm	$D > 0$
	DLØG10(D)	base 10 logarithm	$D > 0$
	DSIN(D)	trigonometric sine	D in radians
	DCØS(D)	trigonometric cosine	D in radians
n	DTAN(D)	trigonometric tangent	D in radians
n	DCØTAN(D)	trigonometric cotangent	D in radians

[n]Not included in ASA Standard FORTRAN IV

DOUBLE PRECISION FUNCTIONS (CONT'D)

CALL	FUNCTION	REMARKS
n DARSIN(D)	arcsine	$-1 \leqslant D \leqslant 1$. Result in radians in 1st or 4th quadrant.
n DARCØS(D)	arccosine	$-1 \leqslant D \leqslant 1$. Result in radians in 1st or 2nd quadrant.
DATAN(D)	arctangent	Result in radians in 1st or 4th quadrant
DATAN2(D,P)	arctangent of D/P	Result in radians in correct quadrant.
nDSINH(D)	hyperbolic sine	
n DCØSH(D)	hyperbolic cosine	
n DTANH(D)	hyperbolic tangent	
n DINT(D)	truncates	
n DFLØAT(I)	converts integer to D.P.	
DBLE(A)	converts real to D.P.	
DMAX1(D,P, ...)	chooses largest	at least 2 arguments required
DMIN1(D,P, ...)	chooses smallest	same as above
DSIGN(D,P)	transfers sign	DABS(D) * (sign of P); $P \neq 0$
n DDIM(D,P)	positive difference	defined: D − DMIN1(D,P)
DMØD(D,P)	remainder of D/P	defined: D − P*DINT(D/P)

REAL FUNCTIONS

CALL	FUNCTION	REMARKS
ABS(A)	absolute value	
SQRT(A)	square root	$A \geqslant 0$
n CBRT(A)	cube root	
EXP(A)	exponential e^a	
ALØG(A)	natural logarithm	$A > 0$
ALØG10(A)	base 10 logarithm	$A > 0$

[n]Not included in ASA Standard FORTRAN IV

REAL FUNCTIONS (CONT'D)

CALL	FUNCTION	REMARKS
SIN(A)	trigonometric sine	A in radians
CØS(A)	trigonometric cosine	A in radians
n TAN(A)	trigonometric tangent	A in radians
n CØTAN(A)	trigonometric cotangent	A in radians
n ASIN(A)	arcsine	$-1 \leqslant A \leqslant 1$. Result in radians in 1st or 4th quadrant
n ARSIN(A)	arcsine	same as above
n ACØS(A)	arccosine	$-1 \leqslant A \leqslant 1$. Result in radians in 1st or 2nd quadrant.
n ARCØS(A)	arccosine	same as above
ATAN(A)	arctangent	Result in radians in 1st or 4th quadrant
ATAN2(A,B)	arctangent of A/B	Result in radians in correct quadrant
n SINH(A)	hyperbolic sine	
n CØSH(A)	hyperbolic cosine	
TANH(A)	hyperbolic tangent	
AINT(A)	truncates	
FLØAT (I)	converts integer to real	
SNGLE(D)	converts D.P. to real unrounded	
REAL(C)	real part of complex	
AIMAG(C)	imaginary part of complex	
CABS(C)	magnitude of complex	
AMAX0(I,J,...)	chooses largest	At least 2 arguments required
AMAX1(A,B,...)	chooses largest	same as above
AMIN0(I,J,...)	chooses smallest	same as above

n Not included in ASA Standard FORTRAN IV

REAL FUNCTIONS (CONT'D)

CALL	FUNCTION	REMARKS
AMIN1(A,B,...)	chooses smallest	at least 2 arguments required
SIGN(A,B)	transfers sign	ABS(A) * (sign of B); $B \neq 0$
DIM(A,B)	positive difference	defined: $A - AMIN1(A,B)$
AMØD(A,B)	remainder of A/B	defined: $A - B * AINT(A/B)$
n RANF(A)	random number generator	A = 0: next RN A < 0: last RN A > 0: new sequence

INTEGER FUNCTIONS

CALL	FUNCTION	REMARKS
IABS(I)	absolute value	
INT(A)	truncates	same as IFIX(A)
IDINT(D)	truncates D.P. to integer	
IFIX(A)	converts real to integer	
MAX0(I,J,...)	chooses largest	at least 2 arguments required
MAX1(A,B,...)	chooses largest	same as above
MIN0(I,J,...)	chooses smallest	same as above
MIN1(A,B,...)	chooses smallest	same as above
ISIGN(I,J)	transfer sign	IABS(I) * (sign of J); $J \neq 0$
IDIM(I,J)	positive difference	defined: $I - MIN0 (I,J)$
MØD(I,J)	remainder of I/J	defined: $I - J * (I/J)$

[n] Not included in ASA Standard FORTRAN IV

7

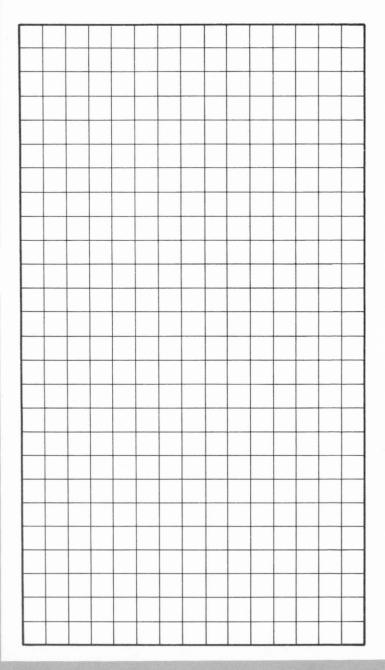

7

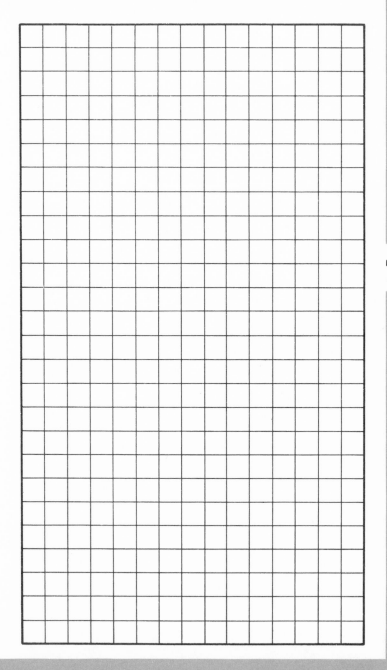

49

TAPE HANDLING STATEMENTS

REWIND   Causes magnetic tape to be rewound to its beginning.

REWIND 2
             └— tape unit number

BACKSPACE   Causes magnetic tape to backspace one record.

BACKSPACE 4
               └—tape unit number

ENDFILE   Causes an "endfile" mark to be placed on the magnetic tape.

ENDFILE 1
               └— tape unit number

Unformatted READ   Causes input of the next record from the magnetic tape into the variables listed in the READ statement. The number of variables may NOT exceed the number of data elements on the tape record.

READ (3) X,Y,I,J
             └— variable list
   └—tape unit number (parentheses required)

Unformatted WRITE   Causes the output of the variables listed in the WRITE statement into the next record of the magnetic tape.

WRITE (4) X,Y,I,J
             └—variable list
   └— tape unit number (parentheses required)

CONTROL AND TRANSFER STATEMENTS

GØ TØ   (unconditional)

GØ TØ 205 ————transfers to this statement number

GØ TØ   (computed) statement numbers (separated by commas)

GØ TØ (7,8,200,32),JELL ◄——— integer variable

JELL=1 =2 =3 =4

transfers to the statement number corresponding to the position named by the value of JELL

GØ TØ   (assigned)

ASSIGN 10 TØ K ———— statement number (from list)

. . . . ————— integer variable

GØ TØ K(13,10,4,87) ——— list of statement numbers – optional (Separated by commas)

transfer is made to the statement number assigned to K

IF   (see Sec. 9)

DØ   (see Sec. 10)

CØNTINUE   A "do nothing" statement to provide program flexibility.

CALL   Used to call a subprogram. (see Sec. 13)

[n]ENTRY   Used in a subprogram as an alternate entry point, other than the beginning of the subprogram. (see Sec. 13)

RETURN   Used in a subprogram to return to the calling program. (see Sec. 13)

PAUSE   Used to interrupt program – operator must restart it.

[n]CALL EXIT Returns control of computer to the monitor.

STØP   Terminates program execution. (Consult computer system manual on whether to use STØP or CALL EXIT prior to END.)

END   Terminates the program -- must be the final statement in a program or subprogram.

[n] Not included in ASA Standard FORTRAN IV

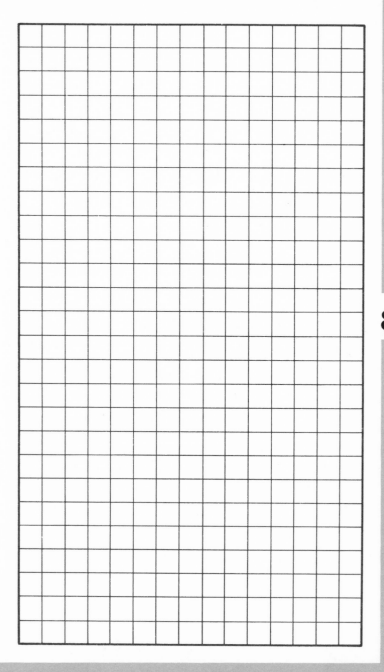

NOTES

LOGICAL IF

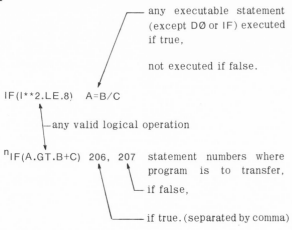

any executable statement
(except DØ or IF) executed
if true,

not executed if false.

IF(I**2.LE.8)   A=B/C

— any valid logical operation

ⁿIF(A.GT.B+C) 206, 207   statement numbers where
program is to transfer,

— if false,

— if true. (separated by comma)

LOGICAL OPERATIONS

RELATIONAL OPERATORS (see table on page 56 for allowable
MIXED MODE operations)

Use: Compare two expressions and give logical result: .TRUE. or
.FALSE.

Fortran	Priority	Meaning	Example
.LT.	5	less than	A.LT.B
.LE.	5	less than or equal to	A+B+C.LE.F
.EQ.	5	equal to	A*10.66+2..EQ.33.0
.NE.	5	not equal to	I.NE.J-3
.GE.	5	greater than or equal to	I+20.GE.K*J*2
.GT.	5	greater than	I.GT.100

ⁿ Not included in ASA Standard FORTRAN IV

LOGICAL OPERATORS (operate with logical expressions and results ONLY)

Fortran	Priority	Meaning	Example	
.NØT.	6	negates	.NØT.TANK	has the value .TRUE. if TANK has the value .FALSE. (TANK must be specified in a LØGICAL type statement)
.AND.	7	both	A.AND.C	has the value .TRUE. if *both* A and B have values .TRUE. otherwise has the value .FALSE.
.ØR.	8	either	A.ØR.C	has the value .TRUE. if either A or C has the value .TRUE. otherwise has the value .FALSE.
Arithmetic operators	1—4	(see Sec 6)		

9

EXAMPLES

IF (A.GT.B.AND.A.GT.C.ØR.B.EQ.C.AND..NØT.TANK) GØ TØ 229

IF (A**2*B.LT.C.ØR.A+D.GE.E.AND.((A/3.54)**J).LE.TAC.AND. (.NØT.TANK)) L=L+1

IF (A.LE.-100.) STØP

Note: 1. parentheses have priority 1 (see Sec 6)

IF

The table below shows valid MIXED MODE operations with relational operators and the mode of the result.

Type (in order of dominance)

C — CØMPLEX

D — DØUBLE PRECISIØN

F — REAL

I — INTEGER

L — LØGICAL

Note: The MODE (type) of an expression is determined by the most dominant element in it.

1st Operand   2nd Operand

		C	D	F	I	L
.LT.	C	—	—	—	—	—
.LE.	D	—	L	L	—	—
.EQ.	F	—	L	L	—	—
.NE.	I	—	—	—	L	—
.GE.	L	—	—	—	—	—
.GT.						

(— invalid or unreliable, depending upon system)

Note:
1. Tests for equality between INTEGER and non-INTEGER variables or expressions are usually *NOT* reliable due to binary conversion.

2. If alphameric variables are to be manipulated or tested, they should all appear under INTEGER variable names to provide valid, reliable results.

ARITHMETIC IF

negative   zero   positive

statement numbers where program is to continue (must be separated by commas)

IF (X+2.3) 210, 211, 212

any valid arithmetic expression (see Sec 6)

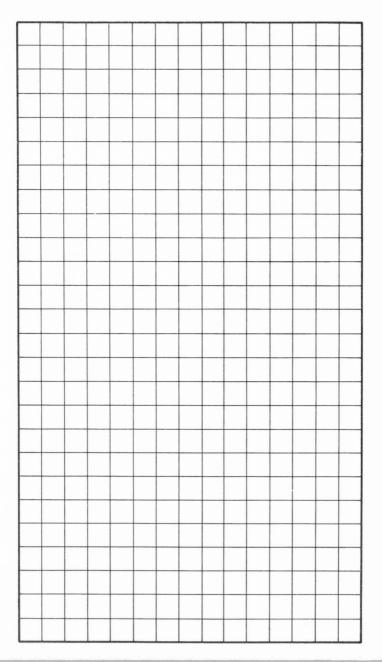

NOTES

REGULAR DØ

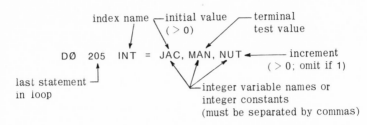

index name — initial value — terminal
(> 0)   test value

DØ   205   INT = JAC, MAN, NUT ←——— increment
                                        (> 0; omit if 1)
last statement —
in loop   integer variable names or
                               integer constants
                               (must be separated by commas)

Means: Do this statement and all succeeding statements in order
including 205 using INT = JAC, then increment so that
INT = INT + NUT and do again all statements through 205,
continue in this manner until INT > MAN, and then go to the
statement immediately following 205.

Note: 1. The last statement in the DØ loop (205 in the example)
MUST be an executable statement.

2. Transfer is allowed OUT of a DØ loop, but not in.

3. If the initial value (JAC) is greater than the terminal
test value (MAN) the loop will be executed once.

NESTED DØ

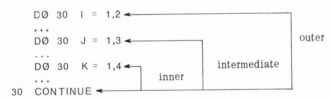

DØ   30   I = 1,2 ←
. . .
DØ   30   J = 1,3 ←   outer
. . .
DØ   30   K = 1,4 ←   intermediate
. . .   inner
30   CONTINUE ←

For each incrementing of the outer DØ loop, the intermediate DØ
loop will increment from its initial to its final value; for each
incrementing of the intermediate DØ loop, the inner DØ loop will
increment from its initial to its final value.

No restrictions are placed on the number of nested DØ loops.

Control can transfer from the inner DØ loops out, but not from the
outer DØ loops in.

IMPLIED DØ   see Sec 12.

DO   58

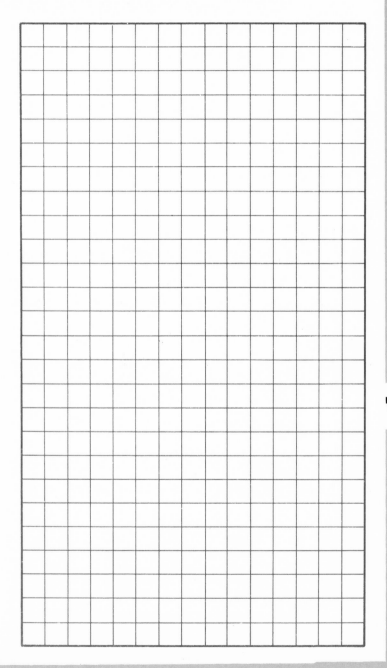

10

OUTPUT DATA – may be obtained from storage by:

1. Unformatted WRITE statement: see Sec. 8

2. Variable format WRITE statement: see Sec. 5, page 37

3. Fixed format WRITE statement (parentheses as shown):

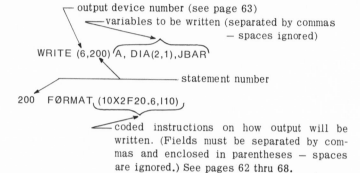

output device number (see page 63)

variables to be written (separated by commas — spaces ignored)

WRITE (6,200) A, DIA(2,1),JBAR

statement number

200 FØRMAT (10X2F20.6,I10)

coded instructions on how output will be written. (Fields must be separated by commas and enclosed in parentheses — spaces are ignored.) See pages 62 thru 68.

Note: 1. Variables and fields MUST correspond in type.

2. If the number of variables listed in the WRITE statement is *less* than the number of fields listed in the FORMAT statement, the extra fields are ignored.

3. If the number of variables listed in the WRITE statement *exceeds* the number of fields listed in the FORMAT statement, the FORMAT statement is used again from its beginning and the remaining variables are written on the next line (or tape record).

1 1

EXAMPLE

This pair of statements:

WRITE (6,400) A,E,I,O,U,L,W ←———— 7 variables
400 FØRMAT (1H ,2F10.2,I5) ←———— 3 data fields

Will cause this printed output:

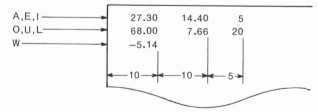

A,E,I ———→ 27.30   14.40   5
O,U,L ———→ 68.00   7.66   20
W ———→   −5.14

|←—10—→|←—10—→|←5→|

OUTPUT

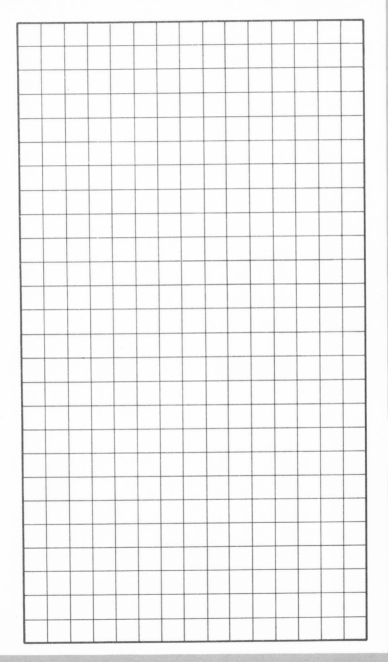

NOTES

OUTPUT FIELDS

	r	t	w.d	required width	use with
Real	4	F	15.5	$w \geq i+d+2$	real, complex
Exponential	1	E	15.8	$w \geq d+7$	real, complex
Double Precision		D	25.15	$w \geq d+7$	D.P.
General (same as E)		G	12.3	$w \geq d+7$ (value $< .1$ or $\geq 10^d$)	real, complex
General (similar to F)		G	12.3	$w \geq d+6$ (value $\geq .1$ & $< 10^d$ — gives d significant digits only)	real, complex
Integer	12	I	5	$w \geq i+1$	integer
[n]Octal	3	O	12	$w \geq i_8$ (negatives in compliment form)	integer, octal
[n]Hexadecimal		Z	8	$w \geq i_{16}$	integer, hex.
Alphameric	5	A	10	variable see example	characters
Alphameric (rt. just.)	7	R	6	variable see example	characters
Logical	2	L	2	$w \geq 1$ ("T" or "F" only)	logical

SCALE FACTOR

	s	P	r	t	w.d	required width
with Real	-2	P	4	F	15.5	$w \geq i+d+2$ (value $\times 10^s$; i may be changed)
with Exp.	3	P	1	E	15.8	$w \geq d+7+s$ $s > 0$ (value unchanged); $w \geq d+7$ $s \leq 0$
with D.P.	O	P		D	25.15	(same as E)
with General	-4	P	3	G	12.3	(same as E when appropriate, or not done)

Notes: Scale factor will apply to all succeeding F, E, D, and G fields within the same format statement until changed or removed with "OP".

Insufficient field width will cause FØRMAT ØVERFLØW error.

s — exponent of scale factor (10^s) — may be −8 thru +8

P — means scale factor

r — repetition number of field (may be omitted if 1)

t — type of field

w — width of field in spaces (1 space = .1 inch)

d — spaces following decimal (omitted for non-real)

i — width of integer, or integer part of real (part left of decimal)

i_8 — width of octal integer

<u>OUTPUT DEVICE NUMBER</u>

Coding varies with different computer systems. Consult your computer's manual.

EXAMPLE OF TYPICAL OUTPUT DEVICE NUMBERS

2	Magnetic tape
4	Console keyboard
6	High-speed printer
8	Card puncher

n Not included in ASA Standard FORTRAN IV

OUTPUT

EXAMPLES OF NUMERIC OUTPUT

ACTUAL VALUES →	-0.32219270	+322.19270	+0.00032219270
		PRINTED OUTPUT	
OUTPUT SPECIFICATION			
3F15.6	-.322193	322.192700	.000322
3E15.6	-3.221927E-01	3.221927E+02	3.221927E-04
3D15.6	-3.221927D-01	3.221927D+02	3.221927D-04
3G15.6	-.322193	322.193	3.221927E-04
2P3F15.6	-32.2219270	32219.270000	.032219
2P3E15.6	-322.19270CE-03	322.192700E+00	322.192700E-06
2P3D15.6	-322.192700D-03	322.192700D+00	322.192700D-06
2P3G15.6	-.322193	322.193	322.192700E-06
-2P3F15.6	-.003222	3.221927	.000003
-2P3E15.6	-.032219E+01	.032219E+04	.032219E-02
-2P3D15.6	-.032219D+01	.032219D+04	.032219D-02
-2P3G15.6	-.322193	322.193	.032219E-02
	←—— 15 spaces ——→	←—— 15 spaces ——→	←—— 15 spaces ——→

(+ sign omitted but space is allowed for it)

OUTPUT SPECIFICATION	PRINTED OUTPUT	ACTUAL VALUES
I20	-3450	-3450
O20	00000000000000000016	14
O20	77777777777777777761	-14
L20	F	.FALSE.
2G10.3	27.5 -5.000E-02	COMPLEX (27.5, -0.05)
E10.3,F10.3	2.750E+01 -.050	COMPLEX (27.5, -0.05)

EXAMPLES OF ALPHAMERIC OUTPUT

ALPHAMERIC OUTPUT – single storage register

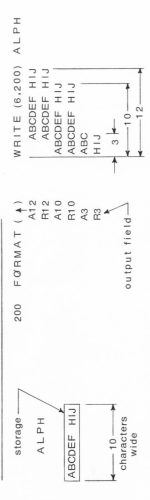

```
          200   FORMAT ( ◄ )        WRITE (6,200) ALPH
                A12                      ABCDEF HIJ
                R12                      ABCDEF HIJ
                A10                      ABCDEF HIJ
                R10                      ABCDEF HIJ
                A3                       ABC
                R3                       HIJ
```

storage
ALPH
ABCDEF HIJ
—10—
characters wide

output field

ALPHAMERIC OUTPUT – multiple storage register

```
DIMENSIØN AMR(2)  201  FORMAT ( ◄ )     WRITE (6,201) AMR
                       2 A12                 ABCDEF HIJ KLM ØPQRST
                       2 R12                 ABCDEF HIJ KLM ØPQRST
                       2 A10                 ABCDEF HIJKLM ØPQRST
                       2 R10                 ABCDEF HIJKLM ØPQRST
                       2 A3                  ABCKLM
                       2 R3                  HIJRST
```

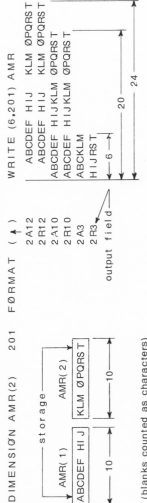

output field

storage
AMR(1) ABCDEF HIJ —10—
AMR(2) KLM ØPQRST —10—

(blanks counted as characters)

PRINTER CARRIAGE CONTROL

The output printer will accommodate 136 (135 printed) columns and and 66 vertical lines of output characters on a standard page (may vary with printer model).

The character in COLUMN ONE of each output line is used for printer carriage control only and is NOT printed — it *should be specified* for each line to prevent accidental carriage control.

EXAMPLE:

207   FØRMAT (1H1,9X4F10.2)
      character in column one is 1

45   FØRMAT (10X4F10.2)
      character in column one is blank

300   FØRMAT (4F10.2)
      character in column one is unknown ◄——— AVOID

6   FØRMAT (7H12 EGGS,4F10.2)
      character in column one is 1 ◄————— NOTE

Character in
column 1	Function
1	start printing on NEW PAGE (on 5th line)
n +	no space — do not shift to next line BEFORE printing
blank	single space — shift to next line BEFORE printing
0	double space — shift two lines BEFORE printing

PUNCHED CARD OUTPUT

The output card puncher will accommodate 80 columns of output characters. The character in column one IS punched since carriage control is not applicable.

[n] Not included in ASA Standard FORTRAN IV

NEW RECORD   slash (/)

The slash causes skipping to the next line (or card, or tape record) whenever it appears in a FØRMAT statement between fields, at the beginning or end of the statement; commas are not needed; it does not apply to succeeding outputs; there is no limit on the number of repetitions per statement.

EXAMPLE:

200   FØRMAT (///13X7HREQUEST/14X5HDATES
      $//10X,14HDAY MO YEAR/)

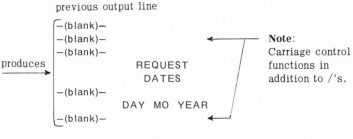

previous output line

```
┌ —(blank)—
│ —(blank)—
│ —(blank)—              Note:
│        REQUEST         Carriage control
│        DATES           functions in
│                        addition to /'s.
│ —(blank)—
│        DAY  MO  YEAR
└ —(blank)—
```
produces

following output line

11

HOLLERITH FIELD   wH <u>characters to be written</u>   (blanks within w are counted; after w are ignored)

[n]symbol varies with computer

' <u>characters to be written</u> '   (blanks within ' ' are counted)

[n]TAB FIELD   Tw   (starts the NEXT field at column w)

BLANK FIELD   wX   (gives w blanks)

HEADINGS CONTAINING OUTPUT DATA

This pair of statements:

    WRITE (6,203) A,B
203 FØRMAT (1H1,10X,6HLENGTH,F10.3,16H FEET / HEIGHT , F8.4,1X,6HINCHES)

Will produce this printed output on a new page:

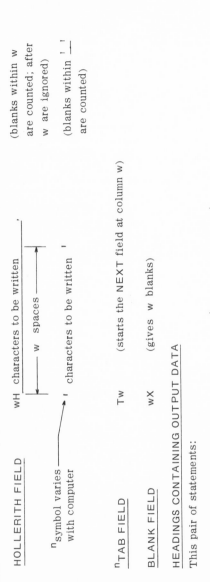

[n] Not included in ASA Standard FORTRAN IV

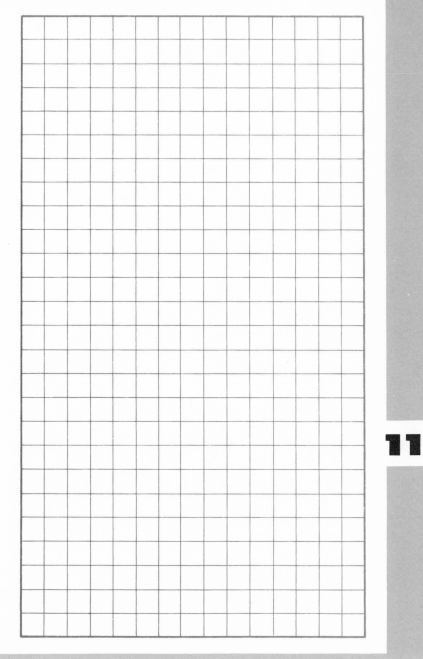

NOTES

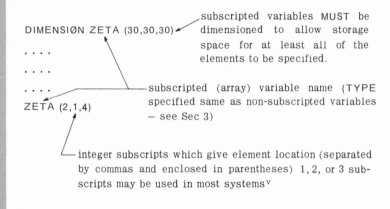

DIMENSIØN ZETA (30,30,30) — subscripted variables MUST be dimensioned to allow storage space for at least all of the elements to be specified.

. . . .

. . . .

. . . .

ZETA (2,1,4) — subscripted (array) variable name (TYPE specified same as non-subscripted variables — see Sec 3)

— integer subscripts which give element location (separated by commas and enclosed in parentheses) 1, 2, or 3 subscripts may be used in most systems[v]

Individual elements may be used as required.

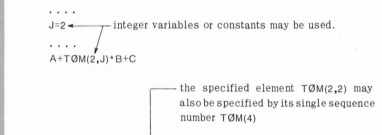

DIMENSIØN TØM (2,3) ——— maximum dimensions

. . . .

J=2 ——— integer variables or constants may be used.

. . . .

A+TØM(2,J)*B+C

— the specified element TØM(2,2) may also be specified by its single sequence number TØM(4)

1, 1	2, 1	1, 2	2, 2	1, 3	2, 3
42.6	27.1	33.0	12.5	0.02	0.50	←—TØM storage

|← maximum dimensions →|

(Note sequence — leftmost subscript indexes fastest)

12

[v] Varies with different computer systems (see Sec. 14)

SUBSCRIPTED (ARRAY) VARIABLES   70

Subscripted variables may be used in DØ loops.

```
DIMENSIØN X(100)
. . . .
X(1)=0.0
. . . .
DØ 25 K=2,100
. . . .                           note use of same integer variable
X(K) = 0.52*X(K−1)+32.2
25    CØNTINUE
```

Subscripted variables may be read in or written out as a complete
array.

```
DIMENSIØN GIN(6,6,6)
. . . .
READ (5,201) GIN          will input all 216 elements
201   FØRMAT (6F10.3)        from 36 data cards with 6
                            elements on each in sequence.
. . . .
WRITE (6,202) GIN
202   FØRMAT (F10.3)          will output all 216 elements,
                            one on each line in sequence.
```

(**Note**: Array sequence — leftmost subscript indexes
fastest)

Subscripted variables may be read in or written out using *explicit*
DØ loops.

```
DIMENSIØN GIN (6,6,6)
. . . .
DØ 32 I=1,6
DØ 32 J=1,6
DØ 32 K=1,6,2
. . . .                          will input and output
READ (5,203) GIN(I,J,K)        every other element:
                               1,1,1 − 1,1,3 − 1,1,5 −
. . . .                          1,2,1 − 1,2,3 − etc.
WRITE (6,204) GIN(I,J,K)
. . . .
32    CØNTINUE
```

12

Arrays may have segments read in or written out using *implied* DØ loops.

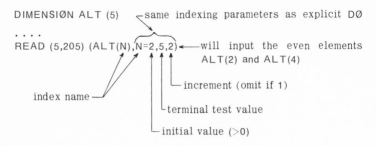

```
DIMENSIØN ALT (5)        same indexing parameters as explicit DØ
. . . .
READ (5,205) (ALT(N),N=2,5,2)    will input the even elements
                                 ALT(2) and ALT(4)

                                 increment (omit if 1)

                                 terminal test value

                                 initial value (>0)

        index name
```

```
DIMENSIØN TØM(2,3)
. . . .
READ (5,210) ((TØM(I,J),J=1,3),I=1,2)
. . . .                    will input:
. . . .                    1,1 − 1,2 − 1,3 − 2,1 − 2,2 − 2,3
WRITE(6,211) ((TØM(I,J),I=1,2),J=1,3)
                           will output:
                           1,1 − 2,1 − 1,2 − 2,2 − 1,3 − 2,3
```

(**Note**: innermost DØ indexes fastest)

```
DIMENSIØN GIN (6,6,6)
. . . .
WRITE (6,204) (((GIN(I,J,K),K=1,6,2),J=1,6),I=1,6)
. . . .              will output every other element:
. . . .              1,1,1 − 1,1,3 − 1,1,5 − 1,2,1 − etc.
. . . .
WRITE (6,204) (((GIN(I,J,K),I=1,6),J=1,6),K=1,6,2)
                     will output every other element,
                     but in different order:
                     1,1,1 − 2,1,1 − 3,1,1 − 4,1,1 − etc.
```

Note position of commas, parentheses, and the order of indexing variables.

12

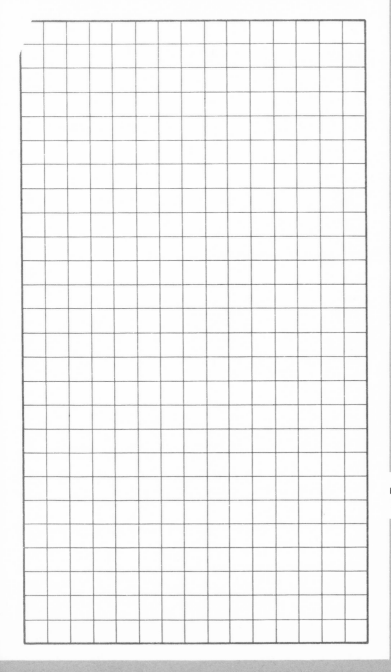

73

	LIBRARY FUNCTIONS (built in)	ARITHMETIC STATEMENT FUNCTION SUBPROGRAM
SOURCE	Provided by computer	Provided by programmer as a single arithmetic statement. May only be used in the program where it is defined.
LOCATION	Computer memory	Within program, prior to any executable statements.
NAME	Pre-assigned by computer. SIN(X)	Assigned by programmer, following by dummy argument list. Mode of name and arithmetic statement must correspond. RAD(D)=D*ACØS(−1.)/180. DEG(R)=R*180./ACØS(−1.)
DUMMY ARGUMENTS	As defined by computer.	Any number, single valued variables.
READ/WRITE	No	No
RESULTS	Single valued constant.	Single valued constant.
CALL	Using the name (with actual argument list) where function value is wanted. H = D * SIN(Y)	Using the name (with actual argument list) where function value is wanted. A = DEG(Y) H = D*SIN(RAD(A))
ACTUAL ARGUMENTS (position & type must correspond with dummy arguments)	Single valued constants or variables; expressions or functions with single valued results. SIN(0.5) SIN(ELEV) ALØG(A+B/C) TAN(ALØG(X))	Single valued constants or variables; expressions or functions with single valued results. ASF(2.3) DEG(ELEV) RAD(A+B/C) SØP(FUNC(D,E,K))
[n]ENTRY	One	One
[n]ENTRY NAME	N/A	N/A
[n]ENTRY CALL	N/A	N/A
RETURN	Automatic	Automatic

[n] Not included in ASA Standard FORTRAN IV
[v] Varies with different computer systems (see Sec. 14)

FUNCTION SUBPROGRAM	SUBROUTINE SUBPROGRAM
Provided by programmer as a complete independent program. May call other independent subprograms.	Provided by programmer as a complete independent program. May call other independent programs.
After main program, prior to any data.	After main program, prior to any data.
Assigned by programmer, followed by dummy argument list. Mode of name and function may be specified, but must correspond. FUNCTIØN J(X,L,INT,Z) REAL FUNCTIØN FUNC(A)	Assigned by programmer, followed by dummy argument list. Mode of name is independent. SUBRØUTINE SUBRØUT(X,Y,Z)
Any number, single valued or array variables (arrays must be dimensioned in BOTH subprogram and calling program), and subprogram names.	
Yes	Yes
Single valued constant	Any number of constants, single valued or array. Arguments of results must be included in argument list.
Using the name (with actual argument list) where function value is wanted C = D + FUNC(T) NN=J(Y,II,N,B)	With CALL statement using subroutine name (with actual argument list). CALL SUBRØUT (T,U,V)
Single valued constants or variables, expressions or functions with single valued results, arrays, or entire subprograms (with EXTERNAL statement).	
FUNC(27.3) (X,J+2,MOD(I,J), D+FUNC(T)) CALL SUBRØUT (T,U,V) EXTERNAL FUNC . . . SIMPSØN (0.,DIST,FUNC) (SIMPSØN integrates FUNC from 0. to DIST.)	
Multiple permitted[v]	Multiple permitted[v]
Assigned by programmer (with or without argument list depending on computer used.) Entry name takes same mode as subprogram name. ENTRY FRED	Assigned by programmer (with or without argument list depending on computer used). Entry name may be assigned any mode. ENTRY JIM
Using entry name (with actual argument list) where function value is wanted. B = D + FRED(R)	With CALL statement using entry name (with actual argument list). CALL JIM(R,U,V)
RETURN statement in subprogram. Multiple returns permitted.	RETURN statement in subprogram. Multiple returns permitted.

Note: Subprograms may call other subprograms, but if subprogram A calls subprogram B, then B may not call A.

SUBPROGRAMS

EXAMPLES:

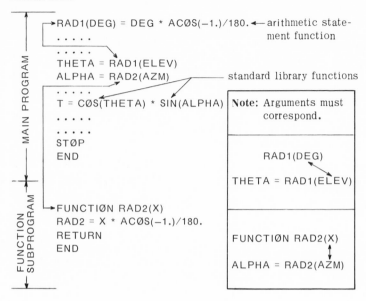

```
RAD1(DEG) = DEG * ACØS(−1.)/180. ←── arithmetic state-
                                          ment function
. . . . .
THETA = RAD1(ELEV)
ALPHA = RAD2(AZM) ──────────── standard library functions
. . . . .
T = CØS(THETA) * SIN(ALPHA)
. . . . .
. . . . .
STØP
END

FUNCTIØN RAD2(X)
RAD2 = X * ACØS(−1.)/180.
RETURN
END
```

MAIN PROGRAM

FUNCTION SUBPROGRAM

Note: Arguments must correspond.

RAD1(DEG)

THETA = RAD1(ELEV)

FUNCTIØN RAD2(X)

ALPHA = RAD2(AZM)

Note: In this example RAD1 and RAD2 accomplish the same thing.

EXAMPLES:

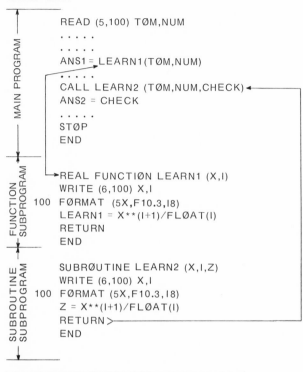

```
            READ (5,100) TØM,NUM
            . . . . .
            . . . . .
            ANS1 = LEARN1(TØM,NUM)
            . . . . .
            CALL LEARN2 (TØM,NUM,CHECK)
            ANS2 = CHECK
            . . . . .
            STØP
            END

            REAL FUNCTIØN LEARN1 (X,I)
            WRITE (6,100) X,I
        100 FØRMAT (5X,F10.3,I8)
            LEARN1 = X**(I+1)/FLØAT(I)
            RETURN
            END

            SUBRØUTINE LEARN2 (X,I,Z)
            WRITE (6,100) X,I
        100 FØRMAT (5X,F10.3,I8)
            Z = X**(I+1)/FLØAT(I)
            RETURN
            END
```

MAIN PROGRAM

FUNCTION SUBPROGRAM

SUBROUTINE SUBPROGRAM

Note: Arguments must correspond.

ANS1 = LEARN1 (TØM,NUM)

REAL FUNCTIØN LEARN1 (X,I)

CALL LEARN2 (TØM,NUM,CHECK)

SUBRØUTINE LEARN2 (X,I,Z)

Note: In this example LEARN1 and LEARN2 accomplish the same thing causing ANS1 to be the same as ANS2.

13

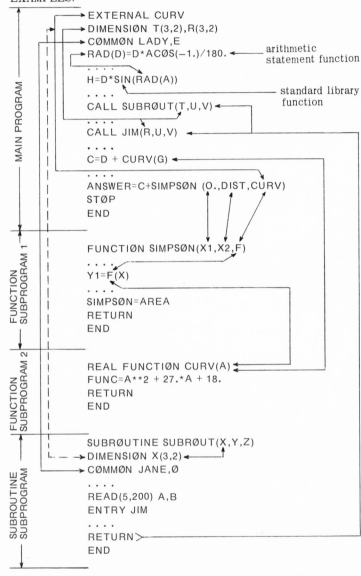

```
            EXTERNAL CURV
            DIMENSIØN T(3,2),R(3,2)
            CØMMØN LADY,E
            RAD(D)=D*ACØS(-1.)/180.        ◄── arithmetic
            . . . .                             statement function
            H=D*SIN(RAD(A))
            . . . .                         ─── standard library
            CALL SUBRØUT(T,U,V) ◄              function
            . . . .
            CALL JIM(R,U,V) ◄
            . . . .
            C=D + CURV(G) ◄
            . . . .
            ANSWER=C+SIMPSØN (O.,DIST,CURV)
            STØP
            END

            FUNCTIØN SIMPSØN(X1,X2,F)
            . . . .
            Y1=F(X)
            . . . .
            SIMPSØN=AREA
            RETURN
            END

            REAL FUNCTIØN CURV(A) ◄
            FUNC=A**2 + 27.*A + 18.
            RETURN
            END

            SUBRØUTINE SUBRØUT(X,Y,Z)
            DIMENSIØN X(3,2) ◄
            CØMMØN JANE,Ø
            . . . .
            READ(5,200) A,B
            ENTRY JIM
            . . . .
            RETURN ►
            END
```

MAIN PROGRAM

FUNCTION SUBPROGRAM 1

FUNCTION SUBPROGRAM 2

SUBROUTINE SUBPROGRAM

(end of record card)

13

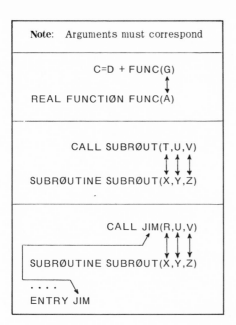

Note: Arguments must correspond

C=D + FUNC(G)
↕
REAL FUNCTIØN FUNC(A)

CALL SUBRØUT(T,U,V)
↕ ↕ ↕
SUBRØUTINE SUBRØUT(X,Y,Z)

CALL JIM(R,U,V)
↕ ↕ ↕
SUBRØUTINE SUBRØUT(X,Y,Z)
. . . .
ENTRY JIM

DATA ◄——————————— | Data, if any, follows the subprograms. It must be in the same order as it will be read by the main and subprograms.

Note: In this example the function CURV is integrated by SIMPSØN from 0 to DIST. (see example on page 80)

13

EXAMPLES OF FUNCTION SUBPROGRAMS
INTEGRATION USING SIMPSON'S METHOD

```
FUNCTIØN SIMPSØN (X1, X2, F)

INC=512
AREA  = 0.
X=X1
Y1=F( X)
DX=( X2−X1) /FLØAT ( INC*2)

DØ 500  I=1, INC
Y2=F( X+DX)
Y3=F( X+2.*DX)
AREA=( Y1+4.*Y2+Y3) *DX/3.+AREA
Y1=Y3
X=X+2.*DX
500      CØNTINUE

SIMPSØN = AREA
RETURN
END
```

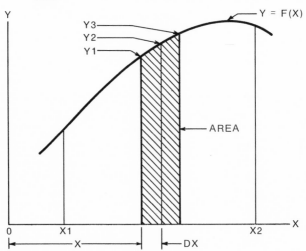

$DX = \dfrac{1}{1024}$ th of the interval X1 to X2

AREA = (Y1+4.*Y2+Y3)*DX/3.

SIMPSØN = the sum of all 512 AREA's

DIFFERENTIATION

```
FUNCTIØN DERIV ( PØINT, DX, F)
DERIV=( F( PØINT+DX/2.) –F ( PØINT–DX/2.) ) /DX
RETURN
END
```

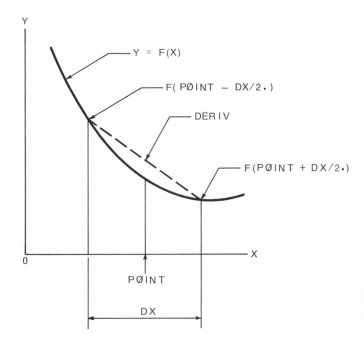

Note: These two subprograms use other subprograms as arguments.

SUBPROGRAMS

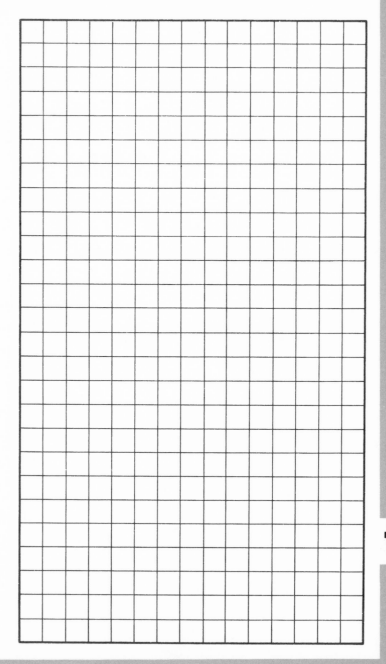

13

	Your computer	Burroughs B-5500	CDC 6000 series	GE 600 series
Max. statement no.		99999	99999	99999
Max. continuation cards		9	no limit	19
Max. characters in variable name		6	7	6
INTEGER − max. digits		11	18	11
INTEGER − max. magnitude		$2^{39}-1$	$2^{59}-1$	$2^{35}-1$
REAL − max. digits		11	14	9
REAL − max. magnitude		10^{69}	10^{308}	10^{38}
DOUBLE PRECISION − max. digits			29	19
DOUBLE PRECISION − max. magnitude			10^{308}	10^{38}
ALPHAMERIC − max. characters		6	10	6
TYPE statement prior to first executable statement		no	yes	yes
Non-ASA mixed MODE operations permitted		no	yes	no
Max. no. of subscripts		3	3	3
Multiple ENTRY to subprograms permitted		no	yes	yes

Honeywell 200	IBM 360-H	IBM 7094	NCR 315	Philco 2000 series	RCA Spectra 70-B	SDS 9300	Univac 1107
99999	99999	32767	99999	32767	99999	99999	32767
9	19	19	19	19	19	no limit	19
6	6	6	no limit	6	6	no limit	6
8	10	11	11	12	10	7	11
$2^{119}-1$	$2^{31}-1$	$2^{35}-1$	$10^{11}-1$	$2^{39}-1$	$2^{31}-1$	$2^{23}-1$	$2^{35}-1$
10	7	9	12	11	7	12	9
10^{99}	10^{75}	10^{38}	10^{150}	10^{616}	10^{75}	10^{77}	10^{38}
20	16	16	21	21	16	19	17
10^{99}	10^{75}	10^{38}	10^{150}	10^{616}	10^{75}	10^{77}	10^{38}
5	4	6		6	4		6
yes	no	no	yes	no	no	no	no
no	yes	no	yes	no	yes	yes	yes
3	7	7	no limit	3	7	no limit	7
no	yes	yes	yes	no	yes	yes	yes

14

ADDRESS   An alphanumeric designation of the storage location of data or information in the computer memory.

ALPHANUMERIC or ALPHAMERIC   A general term for alphabet letters and numeric digits.

ANALOG COMPUTER   Solves problems using CONTINUOUS solutions.

ARGUMENT   Parameters or independent variables to be used by a function or subroutine.

ASSEMBLER   Translates symbolic language instructions into machine language instructions.

BINARY NUMBER SYSTEM   A number system with base two.

BIT   A binary digit.

BOOLEAN ALGEBRA   Propositional calculus using the algebra of truth functions and switching circuits (logic).

BYTE   A specified number of bits.

CHARACTER   A symbol such as: A Z 0 9 $ * + / .

COMPILATION   Transformation of the source program into an object program.

COMPILER   A machine program which processes a source program and transforms it into an object program, expressed in the internal machine language.

CONSTANT   A series of digits representing a numeric quantity.

DATA   Numerical or other forms of quantitative information.

DATA PROCESSOR   A device or system for data processing. Usually such devices are used primarily for sorting or otherwise manipulating information, rather than extensive calculations.

DE-BUGGING   Finding the errors in a program.

DIAGNOSTIC   A message to the programmer, from the computer, that the program contains an error.

15

GLOSSARY   86

DIGIT   A character representing an integer numeric quantity (0 thru 9).

DIGITAL COMPUTER   Solves problems using DISCRETE POINT solutions.

DISC   A magnetic memory unit that looks like a phonograph record.

DRUM   A magnetic memory unit shaped like a cylinder.

EXECUTABLE STATEMENT   A statement that causes computation to take place.

FIXED POINT ARITHMETIC   Computation using INTEGER numbers.

FLOATING POINT ARITHMETIC   Computation using REAL numbers.

FORTRAN LANGUAGE   Statements used by the programmer to describe the operations required for the solution of a problem. A source language.

HOLLERITH   The name of the inventor of the punch code for representing alphanumeric characters.

ITERATION   The repeating of an operation.

JUSTIFY   Setting the end of a string of characters against a specified margin.

LOGICAL OPERATION   An operation using only true and false as values.

MACHINE LANGUAGE   The representation of information in a form the machine can interpret.

MODE (Type)   Kind of arithmetic variables or constants, ie. REAL, INTEGER, etc.

MONITOR   A program to supervise the proper sequencing of programming tasks by the computer.

OBJECT LANGUAGE   Same as machine language.

OCTAL NUMBER SYSTEM   A number system with base eight.

OPERAND   A variable to be operated on by an arithmetic operator (+ − ÷ X).

15

PRECISION   The degree of exactness with which a quantity is specified.

REAL TIME OPERATION   Processing information while the events which produced the information take place.

REGISTER   A temporary storage device or circuit of limited capacity.

SCALING   Shifting the decimal point of a quantity for a specific purpose.

SIGNIFICANT DIGIT   Any digit between the highest non-zero digit and the lowest specified digit in a numerical quantity.

SOURCE LANGUAGE   Language used by the programmer to write the program, such as FORTRAN IV.

SYMBOLIC LANGUAGE   Refers to the location of instructions, data and controls by symbolic names. (ie: variables names, etc.)

STORAGE   Locations in the computer memory for storing data or information.

TRANSFER   To by-pass the normal sequence of statement execution and go to a specified statement.

TYPE   Same as MODE.

VARIABLE   An address name used by the programmer to manipulate data.

WORD   A sequence of digits which is treated by the computer as a unit and which contains a piece of information.

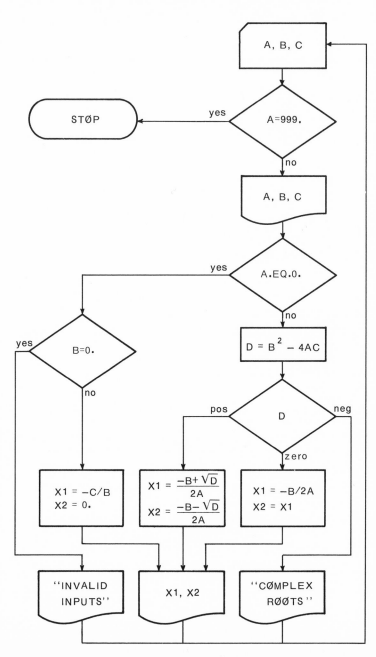

FLOW CHART FOR SOLUTION
TO $AX^2 + BX + C = 0$

A field, 31-35, 62, 65
Alphameric, 21, 35, 65
Arguments, 44-47, 74-81
Arithmetic statement
  function, 74, 76, 78
Arithmetic IF statement, 56
Arithmetic operations, 38-41
Arrays, 70-72
Assigned GO TO statement, 51
ASSIGN statement, 51

BACKSPACE, 50
Binary numbers, 20
Blank COMMON, 25
BLOCK DATA, 27

CALL EXIT statement, 51
CALL statement, 51, 74-81
Card format, 12
Carriage control, 66
Character set, 10
Comments, 12
COMMON, 24-28
COMPLEX numbers, 21, 24
Computed GO TO statement, 51
Computer characteristics, 84-85
Constants, 21
Continuation card, 12
CONTINUE, 51
Control statements, 51

D field, 31-34, 62-64
Data, 12, 79
DATA statement, 26-27
DIMENSION, 25-27
DO statement, 58, 71
DOUBLE PRECISION numbers, 21, 24
Drum card, 8-10

E field, 31-34, 62-64
Elements, 70-72
END FILE, 50
END statement, 51
ENTRY, 51, 74-75, 78
EQUIVALENCE, 25
Exponential numbers, 21

Exponentiation, 39
EXTERNAL, 24, 75, 78-79

F field, 31-34, 62-64
Field specifications, 30-37, 60-68
Fixed-point numbers, 21
Floating-point numbers, 21
Flow chart symbols, 2-3
Flow charts, 89
FORMAT statement, 30, 60
Fortran statements, 12
FUNCTION subprogram, 74-81

G field, 31-34, 62-64
GO TO statement, 51

H field, 36, 68
Hexadecimal numbers, 20-21

I field, 31-35, 62-64
IF statement, 54-56
Implied DO, 72
Identification code, 12
Input statements, 30-37
INTEGER numbers, 21, 24

Key punch machine, 4-9

L field, 31-35, 62-64
Labeled COMMON, 25
Library functions, 44-48, 74-78
LOGICAL, 21, 24
Logical IF statement, 54
Logical operators, 54-56

Magnetic tape, 50
Mixed mode, 38, 40-41
Mode (type), 21, 24-25, 38, 40-41

NAMELIST, 28
Nested DO, 58
Number systems, 20

O field, 31, 62, 64
Octal numbers, 20-21
Output statements, 60-68

P field, 31-34, 62, 64
Paper tape, 17
Parentheses, 39
PAUSE statement, 51
Printer, 66
Priority, 38-39
Program card (drumcard), 8-9
Punch card, 11-13, 66

R field. 31-35, 62-64
READ statement, 30
REAL numbers, 21, 24
Relational operators, 54-55
RETURN, 51, 74-81
REWIND, 50

Scale factor, 31-34, 62-64
Slash in FORMAT statement, 36, 67
Statement FUNCTION, 74, 76, 78
Statement numbers, 12
STOP statement, 51
Subprograms, 74-81

SUBROUTINE, 75, 77-79
Subscripted variables, 70-72

T field, 36, 68
Teletypewriter, 16-18
Transfer statements, 51
Truncation, 38-40, 45, 47
TYPE statement, 21

Unconditional GO TO statement, 51
Unformatted READ, 50
Unformatted WRITE, 50

Variable FORMAT, 37
Variables, 21

WRITE statement, 60

X field, 36, 37, 68

Z field, 31, 62

Catalog

If you are interested in a list of fine Paperback
books, covering a wide range of subjects
and interests, send your name and address,
requesting your free catalog, to:

McGraw-Hill Paperbacks
1221 Avenue of Americas
New York, N.Y. 10020